This book
belongs to

_____

Little Lessons for Life

Written and Illustrated by
Kathy Arbuckle

BARBOUR
PUBLISHING, INC.

© MCMXCVII by Barbour Publishing, Inc.

ISBN 1-57748-285-9

Scripture quotations are from the KING JAMES VERSION of the Bible.

Published by Barbour Publishing, Inc.
P.O. Box 719
Uhrichsville, Ohio 44683
http://www.barbourbooks.com

Member of the
Evangelical Christian
Publishers Association

Printed in China.

F or the
LORD giveth
wisdom: out of his mouth
cometh knowledge and
understanding.

Proverbs 2:6

*For
Christina
and her
sunshine
smile.*

Bible Wisdom for Preschoolers

The fear of the LORD is the beginning of knowledge: but fools despise wisdom and instruction.

Proverbs 1:7

God's special book, the Bible, talks about the "fear of God." "Fearing God" doesn't mean that we should be afraid of God. It means that we should have much respect for God, that we should talk about, talk to, and think of Him as the most important One in the whole world, the whole universe! We should give Him all of our love and learn all that we can about Him. Then we will begin to know true wisdom.

Bible Wisdom for Preschoolers

My son, hear the instruction of thy father, and forsake not the law of thy mother.

Proverbs 1:8

You know that your mommy and daddy are much older and bigger than you and that they know a lot of things. God has given you to your parents so they can take good care of you and teach you the things you need to grow up to be happy and strong. Sometimes they tell you what to do because they know what is best for you and they love you. God loves you, too, and He wants you to obey your parents.

Bible Wisdom for Preschoolers

My son, if sinners entice thee, consent thou not.

Proverbs 1:10

Some people in the world don't love God and don't want to please Him. Instead they do bad things. Many times they will want you to do bad things, too. God says you should not listen to them. Because you love God, you should do what is right, and do the things that make God happy, not sad. Maybe others will see the good things you do and they will want to love God, too.

Bible Wisdom for Preschoolers

But whoso hearkeneth unto me shall dwell safely.

Proverbs 1:33

"Look out!" That is what Joshua said when he saw the red wagon rolling towards his friend Sam. Sam heard the warning and got safely out of the way. The Bible, God's special book, tells us what God says. If you listen to God's Word and do what it says, God will do what is best for you. Just like a caring friend, God is always there to protect you.

Bible Wisdom for Preschoolers

For the LORD giveth wisdom: out of his mouth cometh knowledge and understanding.

Proverbs 2:6

Books are fun to look at and read. You can learn a lot from them. God has His own book called the Bible. In the Bible God has told us many things that help us to live the way He wants us to. You see, God knows everything. Everything He says is right and good, so if you listen to His words, you will learn what is right and good, too.

Bible Wisdom for Preschoolers

Trust in the LORD with all thine heart; and lean not unto thine own understanding. In all thy ways acknowledge him, and he shall direct thy paths.

Proverbs 3:5,6

One morning Meghan thought she could pour the juice herself for her breakfast, so she didn't ask for any help. Meghan didn't know that it would be so hard to pour. Meghan made a big mess. God wants to be in your life everyday. He is there to help you and teach you how to do your best. So talk to Him. Learn about Him. And never be afraid to ask for help.

What can God teach you today?   19

Bible Wisdom for Preschoolers

Honor the LORD with thy sub-
stance, and with the first fruits of
all thine increase: So shall thy
barns be filled with plenty.

Proverbs 3:9,10

Everything you have was given to you
by God. He made everything and owns
the whole world and all that is in it.
Because He has been so good to us we
should give back to Him some of what
He has given us. When you give to God
you show Him that you love Him and
that He is very important to you. After
all, God has given you His very best.

**For whom the LORD loveth he cor-
recteth; even as a father the son in
whom he delighteth.**

Proverbs 3:12

God told Jonah to go tell the people to
stop being wicked, but Jonah didn't
want to obey. So he sailed away on a
boat. While on the boat, a bad storm
came and a big fish swallowed Jonah. It
took three days in the fish's belly for
Jonah to decide to obey God. The fish
spit Jonah out. Jonah told the people
what God had said and a wonderful
thing happened: the wicked people
changed and decided to love God!
Sometimes, you get in trouble for not
obeying your parents, but
they love you and they
want to protect you.

What can God teach you today? 23

Bible Wisdom for Preschoolers

Happy is the man that findeth wisdom, and the man that getteth understanding.

Proverbs 3:13

Sarah has been learning about God. She has learned that God is all-powerful; He is everywhere; He knows everything; and He loves her very, very much. He loves her so much that He gave His Son, Jesus, to be her Savior. Knowing all of these wonderful things makes Sarah happy. Like Sarah, the more you know about God and His wisdom, the happier you will be.

What can God teach you today?

Bible Wisdom for Preschoolers

The LORD by wisdom hath founded the earth; by understanding hath he established the heavens.

Proverbs 3:19

Look at all that is around you. There are animals of every shape and color. They walk, run, swim, or even fly. The plants, trees, and flowers grow and bloom in every color of the rainbow. The earth itself is amazing with its tall mountains, sandy beaches, grassy meadows, and rushing rivers. At night the stars and the moon shine brightly overhead. All of these awesome things were made by God. His knowledge is greater than anyone's.

Bible Wisdom for Preschoolers

Withhold not good from them to whom it is due, when it is in the power of thine hand to do it.

Proverbs 3:27

Sometimes a job is too big for one person to do alone, but two people make it easier. God is pleased when He sees you help someone else. It makes Him happy when you do something good for another person. Even little things like helping to set the table for dinner or helping the neighbor lady rake up the leaves are important ways you can do good for others. When you are a helper you are sharing God's love.

What can God teach you today?   29

Bible Wisdom for Preschoolers

Devise not evil against thy neighbor, seeing he dwelleth securely by thee.

Proverbs 3:29

Do you know your neighbors? Are they your friends? God's Son, Jesus, said we should love our neighbors, all of them. It does not matter if they are rich or poor, young or old, short or tall, boys or girls, or what color skin they have. We should be friendly to all our neighbors because God made them and He loves them.

For wisdom is better than rubies; and all the things that may be desired are not to be compared to it.

Proverbs 8:11

Wisdom is having knowledge and knowing how to use it to please God. Imagine that you found a treasure chest filled with jewels and gold. That treasure would be very valuable, wouldn't it? But God's wisdom is far more valuable than some pretty rocks and shiny metal. Wisdom helps you to live a life that pleases God. And when others see your life they will want to love God, too. Treasures only last for a little while, but God's love lasts FOREVER.

What can God teach you today?

Bible Wisdom for Preschoolers

The mouth of a righteous man is a well of life.

Proverbs 10:11

Every living thing needs water to live: people, plants, animals, and especially fish! Many people get their water from a well. A well is a deep hole in the ground that reaches cool, pure water trapped in the rocks. Some farmers use well water for their animals and fields. So you can see how a well is "life." People who love God can be like "wells of life." They talk about God and share God's love with others. They don't hurt people with mean words, but use their words to please God. You can be a "well of life" for someone today!

What can God teach you today? 35

Bible Wisdom for Preschoolers

The way of the LORD is strength to the upright.

Proverbs 10:29

The Bible tells about a young man named David. One day he went to bring food to his big brothers who were soldiers at a battle. While there, David found himself fighting a giant named Goliath. Now David was still a boy, so he was small compared to Goliath, but he prayed for God to give him the strength to defeat the giant. The Lord answered David's prayer! God will be your strength, too. All you have to do is ask Him for help and He will be there for you.

Bible Wisdom for Preschoolers

A false balance is abomination to the LORD: but a just weight is his delight.

Proverbs 11:1

One day Brian was at the market with his mother buying groceries. He helped her choose five pounds of shiny, red apples. They used the store's scale to weigh the apples and make sure that they were buying five pounds. God wants us to be honest. He wants us to always tell the truth and not lie to each other or to Him. Lies only hurt people. They never help anyone. False words make God sad and angry, but when you are truthful it makes Him happy.

What can God teach you today? 39

Bible Wisdom for Preschoolers

Where no counsel is, the people fall: but in the multitude of counsellors there is safety.

Proverbs 11:14

Lindsay wanted to ride her bike to her friend Bonnie's house. Lindsay asked her mommy if it was okay and then used the map Bonnie had made to show her the way. The directions made it easy for Lindsay to find Bonnie's house. Without them, Lindsay would have gotten lost. It is good to ask for help when you don't know about something. Your family and friends will be glad to help you. And, of course, God is always there to give you His help, too. Just ask Him.

What can God teach you today?   41

Bible Wisdom for Preschoolers

A righteous man regardeth the life of his beast: but the tender mercies of the wicked are cruel.

Proverbs 12:10

You can see Joey filling up his dog's water dish. Joey loves Speckles, his dog, and wants to take very good care of him. He makes sure Speckles has everything he needs to be safe and healthy. We should all do our best to take extra good care of our animals. God made all the puppies, kitties, birds, lizards, mice, horses, and every other animal. They are His gifts to us to care for and love.

Bible Wisdom for Preschoolers

The way of a fool is right in his own eyes: but he that hearkeneth unto counsel is wise.

Proverbs 12:15

Sam crashed his bicycle after riding it over a big jump. Sam's friend Johnny had told him not to ride over it. Johnny said, "It's too big, Sam! You might get hurt!" Sam now knows that he should have listened to his friend. Johnny only wanted to protect Sam. Sometimes your parents or friends tell you not to do something. You should think carefully about what they say and use their words to help you make a smart decision. They love you and only want what is best for you.

Bible Wisdom for Preschoolers

He that speaketh truth sheweth forth righteousness: but a false witness deceit.

Proverbs 12:17

Candace likes the lamp in her room. It makes the whole room bright. When you tell the truth you are like that lamp. Everyone around you can see God's goodness and love by watching how good you are to others. So always be honest with your family, friends, and everybody you know, especially God. It makes Him smile to see you shine with truthfulness.

Every word of God is pure: he is a shield unto them that put their trust in him.

Proverbs 30:5